THE LITTLE
BLACK BOOK OF
SETLISTS

THE LITTLE
BLACK BOOK OF
SETLISTS

FOREWORD BY GLEN MATLOCK

Special Thanks to Glen Matlock

With thanks to Tom Bromley & Verity Muir

First published in Great Britain in 2007 by
Portico Books
10 Southcombe Street
London
W14 0RA

An imprint of Anova Books Company Ltd.

Copyright © Portico Books 2007

Compiled & Edited by Malcolm Croft.

ISBN 9781906032111

10 9 8 7 6 5 4 3 2 1

Printed and bound by SNP Leefung, China.

This book can be ordered direct from the publisher. Contact the marketing department, but try your bookshop first.

www.anovabooks.com

Noel: This is history. This is history.
Right here, right now, this is history.
Liam: No it fookin' isn't, yer daft twat.
This is Knebworth.

Oasis, Knebworth, 10th August 1996

FOREWORD

They will nick.

It's one of the most annoying things that always happens at the start of a gig.

The band come bounding out onto the stage at a club show and the bloke who sets up for you has carefully gaffer-taped the setlist to the floor next to your wedge monitors. The crowd are spilling out over the front of the stage and then you look down to find that somebody has had it away with your running order.

Now this isn't an insurmountable problem, you normally have at least the first couple of songs etched in your mind and the enthusiastic fans can never usually reach the one the drummer has stashed by his stick bag without being turfed off the stage – but it doesn't half take the wind out of your sails!

The name of the game running order wise though, is to come out and hit the crowd squarely between the eyes. I remember debuting 'Anarchy in the UK' at the Lesser Free Trade Hall in Manchester in 1976, and that was indeed just the ticket. Once you have grabbed their attention the task is then to keep it, get 'em rocking and keep them there, take it down ever so slightly after several numbers to give them a slight breather, then crank it back up again.

Do that a few times over the next forty-five minutes and you reach the home straight. The final three or four numbers are when you clinch the deal and get to leave them screaming for more. This though, poses a bit of a dilemma. What are the most happening songs? When you have decided, the trick is to then somehow pepper them throughout your set. Starting strong for a couple, maybe throw in a lesser known track while they are still high on the first few, then following that another happening one and so on until it's classic, classic, classic and then off and where's the rider?

It's always a toss up between what they have paid good money to hear and what you want (maybe a new one or two) to play.

Guess it's a bit like being the bride at a wedding when they wear 'something old, something new, something borrowed and something blue'. Well the 'something blue' could be something a little bit bluesy but it's a pretty good maxim to follow and tends to work for me.

How do you choose what your best songs are?

Experience dear reader, experience.

Once you have the running order nailed, which tends to happen within a few dates at the start of a tour, you might as well stick to it, because if it ain't broke don't fix it. For sure there may be a couple of occasions where one of the band might mis-read what comes next 'cos the fella on the smoke machine has gone a bit bonkers with the button, but you just roll with it, sort it out between yourselves and then it's heads down, see you at the end.

And there you have it – the Matlock guide to taking the roof off.

I would like to leave you with one particular thing I remember though and that was when the Sex

Pistols played London's Crystal Palace a few years back. Out we came to a 25,000 strong crowd all eagerly anticipating the show. To all intents and purposes it looked from the stage that the whole of the front few rows of the crowd had placed a bet on what the opening salvo would be...

'Anarchy'? 'Vacant'? 'Bodies'?

Nah, Hawkwind's 'Silver Machine'!

The look on their faces was priceless.

Should have put a bet on myself...

Glen Matlock, London, May 2007

INTRODUCTION

Welcome to the *Little Black Book of Setlists* – your definitive guide to the concerts that shaped the course of rock 'n' roll.

In compiling this little book, much blood was shed, many people walked out in utter disgust and many late nights turned into early mornings trying to figure out what makes a classic show better than just 'all right'. In your hands is the result of our research (and heated debate) into the biggest and the loudest, the first and the last, the most remarkable and the most intimate, and the gigs where you just think, 'Shit, I wish I'd gone to that.'

The following concerts were chosen not only for their size or because clichéd rock history has led us to believe they were that great (although it's often true), they were chosen because we've seen how culture, other bands and the audience responded to such events and how they ultimately changed the musical landscape around us. Classic shows encapsulate why we connect with certain bands and songs, and why, despite the overpriced tickets and beer and underage children moshing out of time, you still can't wait to see your favourite bands walk out on stage.

Now, where did we put that ticket stub for the cloakroom …

Woody Guthrie

US Department of the Interior, Washington DC
22nd March 1940

Hard Times
Pretty Boy Floyd
They Laid Jesus Christ In His Grave
Jolly Banker
I Ain't Got No Home
So Long, It's Been Good To Know You
Talking Dust Bowl Blues
Do-Re-Mi
Rye Whiskey
Goin' Down That Road Feeling Bad
Dust Storm Disaster
Dust Pneumonia Blues

Alan Lomax, assistant in charge of the Archive of American Folk Song at the Library of Congress, first heard Woody Guthrie in March 1940. Guthrie was then commissioned by the US Department of the Interior to write songs for the Columbia River and the building of the Bonneville dam. He wrote twenty-six songs in thirty days.

Billie Holiday

Flamingo Club, London
14th February 1954

Blue Moon
Fine And Mellow
Willow Weep For Me
Too Marvellous For Words
Lover Man (Oh, Where Can You Be?)

Alongside her Royal Albert Hall performance, Holiday's Valentine's Day performance at the Flamingo has gone down as one of the all-time greats. With Carl Drinkhard on piano, Holiday summed up her performance with the song 'Too Marvellous For Words'.

Miles Davis

Newport Jazz Festival, Newport, Rhode Island
17th July 1955

Hackensack
Round Midnight
Now's The Time

The defining Miles Davis gig. Performing Theolonius Monk's 'Round Midnight' (with Monk on piano), Davis played this solo to high praise and never looked back. This performance alone re-awakened critical interest in him and led to the formation of his quintet with John Coltrane and signing to Columbia records.

3

Elvis Presley

Robinson Memorial Auditorium, Little Rock, Arizona

16th May 1956

Heartbreak Hotel
Long Tall Sally
I Was The One
Money Honey
I Got A Woman
Blue Suede Shoes
Hound Dog

This gig reflects Elvis's pre-draft period and considered the most productive period of Elvis's career before the movies, the jumpsuit and the glazed doughnuts. The Hillbilly Cat (as he was originally known), with those swinging hips and rockabilly baritone, was a completely original and mesmerizing artist unseen before.

Buddy Holly

Winter Dance Party, The Surf Ballroom, Clear Lake, Iowa
2nd February 1959

Gotta Travel On
It Doesn't Matter Anymore
Peggy Sue
That'll Be The Day
It's So Easy
Everyday
Oh Boy
Early In The Morning
Rave On

'The day the music died' sang Don McLean on 'American Pie'. Following the Surf's annual 'Winter Dance Party' on 2nd February 1959, a plane – on its way to another performance – crashed five miles north of Clear Lake, killing not only the pilot but its three famous passengers – Buddy Holly, J.P. 'The Big Bopper' Richardson, and Ritchie Valens.

Frank Sinatra
(w/ Red Norvo Quintet)

West Melbourne Stadium, Melbourne
1st April 1959

Perdido (Instrumental)
Between The Devil And The Deep Blue Sea
I Could Have Danced All Night
Just One Of Those Things
I Get A Kick Out Of You
At Long Last Love
Willow Weep For Me
I've Got You Under My Skin
Moonlight In Vermont
The Lady Is A Tramp
Sinatra Speaks
Angel Eyes
Come Fly With Me
All The Way
Dancing In The Dark
One For My Baby (And One More For
The Road)
All Of Me
On The Road To Mandalay
Night And Day

Sinatra's Australian two-date Australian tour in 1959 were notable particularly for the singer's finest, and wildest, performances. Just as he begun 'I've Got You Under My Skin' a woman in the audience screamed. Sinatra responded coolly with 'Get your hands off that broad!'

Muddy Waters

I Got My Brand On You
(I'm Your) Hoochie Coochie Man
Baby Please Don't Go
Soon Forgotten
Tiger In Your Tank
I Feel So Good
I've Got My Mojo Working
Goodbye Newport Blues

Waters, backed by a band including Otis Spann, James Cotton, and Pat Hare played with all the zest you'd expect from the great man himself and legendary session players. In 2003, the live album of this exact performance was ranked Number 348 in *Rolling Stone's* list of the 500 greatest albums of all time.

Judy Garland

Carnegie Hall, New York
23rd April 1961

Overture • The Trolley Song •
Over The Rainbow • The Man That Got Away
When You're Smiling (The Whole World Smiles
With You) • Almost Like Being In Love •
This Can't Be Love • Do It Again • You Go To
My Head • Alone Together • Who Cares (So
Long As You Care For Me) • Puttin' On The Ritz
• How Long Has This Been Going On? • Just You,
Just Me • The Man That Got Away •
San Francisco • I Can't Give You Anything
But Love • That's Entertainment • Come Rain Or
Come Shine • You're Nearer • A Foggy Day •
If Love Were All • Zing! Went The Strings Of
My Heart • Stormy Weather • You Made Me
Love You/For Me & My Gal/The Trolley Song •
Rock-A-Bye Your Baby • Over The Rainbow •
Swanee • After You've Gone • Chicago •

Judy Garland's effortless star appeal became unde-
niable with this classic Carnegie Hall performance.
'Over The Rainbow' was even played twice for good
measure. So good was this show, Rufus Wainwright
're-performed' the entire set back at the Carnegie
Hall in June 2006.

Rolling Stones

Marquee Club, London
12th July 1962

Kansas City
Honey, What's Wrong?
Confessin' the Blues
Bright Lights Big City
I Believe I'll Dust My Broom
Down The Road Apiece
I Want You To Love Me
Bad Boy
I Ain't Got You
Hush Hush
Ride 'Em On Down
Back In The USA
Kind Of Lonesome
Blues Before Sunrise
Big Boss Man
Don't Stay Out Night
Tell Me That You Love Me
Happy Home

The Rolling Stones's very first concert. Five men shaking their moneymakers with the world barely taking notice. Compared to today's Stones – with giant record-breaking tours in front of millions of fans – this tiny gig in front of a handful of people must all seem so long ago.

James Brown

Apollo Theatre, New York
24th October 1962

I'll Go Crazy
Try Me
I Don't Mind
Lost Someone
Please, Please, Please
You've Got The Power
I Found Someone
Why Do You Do Me?
I Want You So Bad
I Love You, Yes I Do
Why Does Everything Happen To Me
Bewildered
Please, Please, Please
Night Train

James Brown's *Live At The Apollo* performance has become one of the best live recordings ever commited to tape. This was the defining show af Brown's early career.

Rolling Stones

New Victoria Theatre, London
29th September 1963

Poison Ivy
Fortune Teller
Come On
Money
Route 66
Roll Over Beethoven
Talking Bout You
Bye Bye Johnny

In a dream line-up of bands (supporting Bo Diddley, Little Richard and the Everly Brothers) this was the Rolling Stones's opening show of their first UK tour.

Dean Martin

Sands Hotel, Las Vegas
4th February 1964

Bourbon From Heaven/It's Alright With Me
June In January
You Must Have Been A Beautiful Baby
Memories Are Made Of This
That's Amoré
You Made Me Love You/It Had To Be
You/Nevertheless/I'm In Love With You/On A
Slow Boat To China
Volare/An Evening In Rome
Mr. Wonderful

Ol' Dino at the Sands in his prime. This rat pack crooner and Sinatra's crony could never be accused of being the most energetic performer but his laid-back charm and ease with an audience always shone through.

The Beach Boys

Memorial Auditorium, California

1st April 1964

Little Honda
Papa-Oom-Mow-Mow
The Little Old Lady From Pasadena
Hushabye
Hawaii
Let's Go Trippin'
The Wanderer
Surfer Girl
Monster Mash
Be True To Your School
Graduation Day
Surfin' USA
Don't Back Down
Don't Worry Baby
Wendy
I Get Around
Fun, Fun, Fun

One of the Beach Boys' earliest shows – the toils of drug abuse and in-band squabbling seem so far off judging by the innocence of 'Monster Mash', 'Be True to Your School' and 'Graduation Day' in the set.

13

Bob Dylan

Newport Folk Festival, Newport, Rhode Island
25th July 1965

Maggie's Farm
Like A Rolling Stone
Phantom Engineer
It's All Over Now, Baby Blue
Mr. Tambourine Man

The moment Dylan went 'electric'. Before this
headline show, Dylan told no more people than
necessary about his plans for an electric
performance, so when the group turned up the
volume for 'Maggie's Farm', the traditional folk fans
in the audience reacted negatively. After playing
three songs, Dylan walked off – only to return with
his acoustic guitar for the final songs.

The Beatles

Twist And Shout
She's A Woman
I Feel Fine
Dizzy Miss Lizzy
Ticket To Ride
Everybody's Trying To Be My Baby
Can't Buy Me Love
Baby's In Black
I Wanna Be Your Man
A Hard Day's Night
Help!
I'm Down

As legendary gigs go, the Beatles at Shea Stadium is top of the list. This was the first stadium rock concert and in front of a then record sell-out crowd of 55,600. Performing on a makeshift stage (where second-base would normally be) the band earned a whopping $160,000 for their 30-minute set.

The NME Poll-winner's Concert

Wembley Empire Pool, London
1st May 1966

Substitute • My Generation (The Who)
You Don't Have To Say You Love Me
(Dusty Springfield)
Keep On Running (Spencer Davis Group)
Sha-La-La-La-Lee (Small Faces)
The Sun Ain't Gonna Shine Anymore
(The Walker Brothers)
Shapes Of Things (The Yardbirds)
The Last Time • Play With Fire • Satisfaction
(The Rolling Stones)
I Feel Fine • If I Needed Someone • I'm Down
(The Beatles)

In 1966, before 10,000 of England's screaming teenagers, quite possibly the greatest gig ever nearly didn't take place. Due to a heated argument between John Lennon and Mick Jagger – over who headlined the *previous year's* concert – this Poll-winner's show was never allowed to be captured live on TV. The Beatles never played live before a British audience again.

Bob Dylan (w/ The Hawks)

Manchester Free Trade Hall
17th May 1966

She Belongs To Me
Fourth Time Around
Visions Of Johanna
It's All Over Now, Baby Blue
Desolation Row
Just Like A Woman
Mr. Tambourine Man

With The Hawks:

Tell Me, Momma
I Don't Believe You (She Acts Like We Never
Have Met)
Baby, Let Me Follow You Down
Just Like Tom Thumb's Blues
Leopard-Skin Pill-Box Hat
One Too Many Mornings
Ballad Of A Thin Man
Like A Rolling Stone

The infamous 'electric' Dylan gig and quite possibly the most discussed concert in the history of rock and roll. Audience member John Cordwell heckled Dylan with taunts of 'Judas' – a comment on Dylan's betrayal of his folk roots by playing an electric guitar. Dylan responded with 'I don't believe you, you're a liar', then instructed the band to 'play fucking loud'.

The Beatles

Candlestick Park, San Francisco
29th August 1966

Rock And Roll Music
She's A Woman
If I Needed Someone
Day Tripper
Baby's In Black
I Feel Fine
Yesterday
I Wanna Be Your Man
Nowhere Man
Paperback Writer
Long Tall Sally

Following Lennon's 'Bigger than Jesus' comment, and the demoralising incidents in the Phillipines the Beatles were through with touring. This was their last performance. Not that it mattered – they couldn't hear a thing they were playing through all the hysterical screaming.

Otis Redding

Shake
Respect
I've Been Loving You Too Long
Satisfaction
Try A Little Tenderness

Otis Redding demonstrated his expansion of reper-
toire by performing a stunning version of
'Satisfaction' (still Jagger's favourite cover of a
Stones record) to an audience predominantly made
up of pop and rock fans.

Jimi Hendrix

Monterey International Pop Festival, Monterey, California

18th June 1967

Killing Floor
Foxy Lady
Like A Rolling Stone
Rock Me Baby
Hey Joe
Can You See Me
The Wind Cries Mary
Purple Haze
Wild Thing

This gig was one of the live experiences of the late 1960s. The set culminated with Jimi taking his Fender Stratocaster and setting it on fire during, somewhat aptly, 'Wild Thing'. Bandmates Mitch Mitchell and Noel Redding looked on approvingly. This was also the Experience's first ever show in the USA.

Chuck Berry

Fillmore Auditorium, San Francisco

27th June 1967

Rockin' At The Fillmore
Everyday I Have The Blues
C.C. Rider
Driftin' Blues
Feelin' It
Flying Home
Hoochie Coochie Man
It Hurts Me Too
Good Morning Little School Girl
Fillmore Blues
Reelin' And Rockin'
My Ding-A-Ling
Johnny B. Goode

Berry's version of 'My Ding-A-Ling' bizarrely went to the UK Number One spot in 1972 though he was playing it live many years before. For this particular show, Berry was backed by the Steve Miller Band – later to find fame on their own.

Johnny Cash

Folsom State Prison, Folsom, California
January 13th 1968

Folsom Prison Blues
Busted
Dark As A Dungeon
I Still Miss Someone
Cocaine Blues
25 Minutes To Go
Orange Blossom Special
The Long Black Veil
Send A Picture Of Mother
The Wall
Dirty Old Egg-Suckin' Dog
Flushed From The Bathroom Of Your Heart
Joe Bean
Jackson (Duet with June Carter)
Give My Love To Rose
I Got Stripes (Duet with June Carter)
The Legend Of John Henry's Hammer
Green, Green Grass Of Home
Greystone Chapel

In 2003, this gig was one of fifty recordings chosen by the Library of Congress to be added to the National Recording Registry. The final song, 'Greystone Chapel', was written by inmate Glen Sherley. As the myth goes, a Reverend asked Cash to listen to a tape of Sherley singing the song. Upon hearing it, Cash rushed to include it on the live set the next night.

Elvis Presley

Comeback Special, International Hotel, Las Vegas
27th June 1968

Trouble / Guitar Man
Heartbreak Hotel
Hound Dog
All Shook Up
Can't Help Falling In Love
Jailhouse Rock
Don't Be Cruel
Blue Suede Shoes
Love Me Tender
Baby What You Want Me To Do
Trouble / Guitar Man
Sometimes I Feel Like A Motherless Child /
Where Could I Go But To The Lord /
A Little Less Conversation
If I Can Dream
When It Rains, It Really Pours
Heartbreak Hotel
Love Me
Blue Suede Shoes
Are You Lonesome Tonight?

Reunited with longtime band members Scotty Moore and D.J. Fontana, Elvis's performance here is a real *tour de force*. With its blending of the old Elvis into something new, this '68 comeback re-established Elvis – dressed in an especially made black leather outfit – at the peak of his career.

The Doors

The Round House, London
6th September 1968

Five To One
Break On Through
When The Music's Over
Alabama Song
Back Door Man/Crawling King Snake
Spanish Caravan
Love Me Two Times
Light My Fire
Unknown Soldier
Soul Kitchen
Little Game/The Hill Dwellers/Not To Touch
The Earth
Hello I Love You
Moonlight Drive/ Horse Latitudes
Money

The Doors' first gig on UK soil. The band played an early and late show, which while uncommon now, was quite a regular demand of venues in the 1960s.

Cream

White Room
Politician
I'm So Glad
Sitting On Top Of The World
Crossroads
Toad
Spoonful
Sunshine Of Your Love
Stepping Out

The band's farewell show, the end of their last tour and the last time they would play together until reforming 37 years later.

The Beatles

Apple Corps Rooftop, London
30th January 1969

Get Back
Get Back
Don't Let Me Down
I've Got A Feeling
The One After 909
Dig A Pony
God Save The Queen
I've Got A Feeling
Don't Let Me Down
Get Back

Even if it can't be classified as a proper concert, this
celebrated rooftop gig was the Beatles' last ever performance as a group. The 42-minute show, with
Billy Preston on keys, and on a freezing cold rooftop
in January brought part of London to a standstill.
The police, as always, pulled the plug.

Johnny Cash

San Quentin Prison, San Quentin, California
24th February 1969

Big River
I Still Miss Someone
Wreck Of The Old '97 L
I Walk The Line
Darlin' Companion
I Don't Know Where I'm Bound
Starkville City Jail
San Quentin
Wanted Man
Boy Named Sue
Peace In The Valley
Folsom Prison Blues
Ring Of Fire
He Turned The Water Into Wine
Daddy Sang Bass
Old Account Was Settled Long Ago
Folsom Prison Blues/I Walk The Line/Ring Of Fire

Johnny Cash's San Quentin performance has been called 'the angriest, toughest most punk rock album of all time'. Cash was down and out in the times preceding this gig and came back with a song, 'San Quentin', as an attempt to initiate prison reform in America.

Pink Floyd

South Bank Queen Elizabeth Hall,
London 12th May 1967

Dawn
Matilda Mother
Flaming
Games For May
Bicycle
Arnold Layne
Candy And A Currant Bun
Pow R Toc H
Interstellar Overdrive
Bubbles
Ending
Lucifer Sam

Arguably, Pink Floyd's breakthrough and most influential gig. The band promised the audience 'space age relaxation for the climax of spring; with electronic compositions, colour and image projections and the Pink Floyd'. Unsuprisingly, perhaps, the group were banned from playing there ever again. To commemorate Syd Barrett's death this gig was 'recreated' in May 2007 with Graham Coxon, Terry Edwards and Robyn Hitchcock performing.

28

Led Zeppelin

Surrey University, Guildford
15th October 1968

Train Kept A Rollin'
I Can't Quit You
As Long As I Have You
How Many More Times
Pat's Delight

Led Zeppelin's debut show as Led Zeppelin – a name chosen by Keith Moon when predicting that the band would go down like a 'lead zeppelin'. Originally named 'The New Yardbirds', the group signed a $200,000 recording deal (then a record-signing for a new band) just one month after this gig.

Rolling Stones

Hyde Park, London
5th July 1969

I'm Yours and I'm Hers
Jumpin' Jack Flash
Mercy Mercy
Down Home Girl
Stray Cat Blues
No Expectations
I'm Free
Loving Cup
Love In Vain
(I Can't Get No) Satisfaction
Honky Tonk Woman
Midnight Rambler
Street Fighting Man
Sympathy For The Devil

Just two days before this gig, Brian Jones was found dead. As a tribute to their former bandmate, the Stones released 1,000 white moths into the air. However, due to the baking heat most of the moths died in their boxes.

Rolling Stones

Altamont Speedway, Livermore, California
12th December 1969

Jumpin' Jack Flash
Carol
Sympathy For The Devil
The Sun Is Shining
Stray Cat Blues
Love In Vain
Under My Thumb
Brown Sugar
Midnight Rambler
Live With Me
Gimme Shelter
Little Queenie
Satisfaction
Honky Tonk Women
Street Fighting Man

At Altamont Speedway the Stones played a free concert (for the intention of inclusion in the movie *Gimme Shelter*) and a staggering 400,000 people turned up. Chaos ensued when a Stones fan was killed by the Hell's Angels motorcyle club (employed ironically as security). Lost among all the madness, this show was actually the live debut of 'Brown Sugar'.

The Velvet Underground

The Family Dog, San Francisco
11th August 1969

I'm Waiting For The Man
It's Just Too Much
What Goes On
I Can't Stand It
Some Kinda Love
Foggy Notion
Femme Fatale
After Hours
I'm Sticking With You
Sunday Morning
Sister Ray
Follow The Leader
White Light/White Heat
Venus In Furs
Heroin
Sister Ray
Rock And Roll
New Age
Over You
Black Angel's
Death Song
I'm Waiting For The Man
Ride Into The Sun
Sister Ray/Foggy Notion

By this gig John Cale had left the Velvets, but their
fanbase had grown enough for many of their loyal
fans to bring their own recording equipment to cap-
ture the band live – as they did with this energetic
bootlegged gig.

Santana

Woodstock Festival, Max Yasgur's Farm, New York State
16th August 1969

Waiting
You Just Don't Care
Savor
Jingo
Persuasion
Soul Sacrafice
Fried Neckbones

The fusion of blues with Latin rhythms provided a unique sound for the crowd at Woodstock. Mike Carabello and Jose Areas added a percussive flourish to the drumming of a sixteen-year-old Mike Shrieve. Santana released *Santana* on the back of this now-legendary performance.

Jimi Hendrix

Woodstock Festival, Max Yasgur's Farm, New York State
19th August 1969

Message To Love
Hear My Train A Comin'
Spanish Castle Magic
Red House
Master Mind
Here Comes Your Lover Man
Foxy Lady
Beginning
Izabella
Gypsy Woman
Fire
Voodoo Child/Stepping Stone
Star Spangled Banner
Purple Haze
Woodstock Improvisation/Villanova Junction
Hey Joe

Arguably one of the most inspiring sets ever played. Including the magnificent rendition of 'Star Spangled Banner' – raw and grand all at the same time. Insisting on being the festival's final performer, Hendrix didn't take the stage until 9am on Monday morning, playing for 2 hours to, no doubt, a very hungover audience.

John Lennon

Toronto Rock 'n' Roll Revival Festival, Toronto
13th September 1969

Blue Suede Shoes
Money
Dizzy Miss Lizzy
Yer Blues
Cold Turkey
Give Peace A Chance
Don't Worry Kyoko (Mummy's Only Looking
For Her Hand In The Snow)
John John (Let's Hope For Peace)

As a supergroup-consisting of Lennon and Ono, Eric Clapton on guitars, Klaus Voorman on bass, and Alan White on drums – you would just expect this gig to be magnificent. This was also Lennon's first show without the other Beatles.

Miles Davis

Hammersmith Odeon, London
1st November 1969

Directions
Bitches Brew
It's About That Time
I Fall In Love Too Easily
Sanctuary
No Blues
Paraphernalia
Masqualero

Miles Davis. The King of Cool. London. 1969. At the end of the swinging sixties, Davis was beginning his 'fusion' phase of popular rock music and jazz. While assembling more fans in this period than he had ever before, some accused him of selling out.

The Who

Heaven And Hell
I Can't Explain
Fortune Teller
Tattoo
Young Man Blues
Substitute
Magic Bus
Happy Jack
I'm A Boy
A Quick One, While He's Away
Summertime Blues
Shakin' All Over
My Generation
Overture
It's A Boy
1921
Amazing Journey

The legendary Who performance. The epitome of rock and roll summed up in one classic setlist, and a show that the band revisited, and recreated, thirty years later.

Fleetwood Mac

Sporthalle, Bøblingen, Germany
15th February 1970

Black Magic Woman
Before The Beginning
Like It This Way
Only You
Madison blues
Rattlesnake Shake
Searching For Madge
Rattlesnake Shake
Got To Move
Worried Life Blues
World In Harmony
I Can't Hold Out
Oh Well
Coming Your Way

The tour where, famously, founding member Peter Green quit Fleetwood Mac after going on a three-day LSD binge. Green admitted he simply 'went on a trip, and never came back'.

The Doors

Isle of Wight Festival
29th August 1970

Back Door Man
Break On Through
When The Music's Over
Ship Of Fools
Roadhouse Blues
Light My Fire
The End
Across The Sea
Away In India
Crossroads
Wake Up
The End

Not much can beat seeing the Doors live at the Isle of Wight Festival in 1970. Whether you were a Doors fan or not, this gig went a long way to mythologising the band's status and Jim Morrison's tag as American poet and provocative performer.

The Who

Isle of Wight Festival
29th August 1970

Heaven And Hell • I Can't Explain •
Young Man Blues • I Don't Even Know Myself •
Water • Overture • It's A Boy • 1921 •
Amazing Journey • Sparks • Eyesight To The Blind
• Christmas • The Acid Queen • Pinball Wizard •
Do You Think its Alright • Fiddle About •
Tommy Can You Hear Me • There's A Doctor •
Go To The Mirror • Smash The Mirror •
Miracle Cure • I'm Free • Tommy's Holiday
Camp • We're Not Gonna Take It • Summertime
Blues • Shaking All Over • Spoonful • Twist And
Shout • Substitute • My Generation • Magic Bus

Arriving on stage at 3am, the band played for two hours in a whirlwind 33-song setlist. Pete Townsend kept a tumbler of whisky by the stage, just in case he played the windmill action badly and cut the tips of his fingers. The whisky would help sterilise his fingers.

Jimi Hendrix

Isle of Wight Festival

30th August 1970

God Save The Queen
Sergeant Pepper's Lonely Hearts Club Band
Spanish Castle Magic
All Along The Watchtower
Machine Gun
Lover Man
Voodoo Chile
Freedom
Red House
Dolly Dagger
Midnight Lightnin'
Foxy Lady
Message To Love
Hey Baby (Land of the New Rising Sun)
Easy Rider
Hey Joe
Purple Haze
Voodoo Chile (slight return)
In From The Storm

Jimi Hendrix has, of course, played many magnificent shows but this Isle of Wight performance with Mitch Mitchell and Billy Cox (replacing The Experience) was one which many people still talk about today. Hendrix would be dead within three weeks.

Aretha Franklin

Fillmore West, San Francisco, California

5th March 1971

Respect
Love the One You're With
Bridge Over Troubled Water
Eleanor Rigby
Make It With You
Don't Play That Song
Dr. Feelgood
Spirit In The Dark
Spirit In The Dark (Reprise)
Somebody's Hand

This is the only ever date that Aretha Franklin played the legendary Fillmore venue in San Francisco. Her performance was supported by Billy Preston, Ray Charles and King Curtis and the Kingpins.

The Beach Boys

Fillmore East, New York

27th April 1971

Searchin'
Riot In Cell Block #9
Good Vibrations
I Get Around
Help Me Rhonda
Okie From Muskogee
Johnny B. Goode

The early 1970s weren't the best of times for the Beach Boys but this show, in the middle of all the madness, was triumphant. Following a bizarre, but equally enjoyable jam with the Grateful Dead (after their three hour set!) the Boys took to the completely silent stage. Not sure what to expect, and after an initially frosty response from the audience, the gig ended with overwhelming applause.

Carole King

Carnegie Hall, New York
18th June 1971

I Feel The Earth Move
Home Again
After All This Time
Child Of Mine
Carry Your Load
No Easy Way Down
Song Of Long Ago
Snow Queen
Smackwater Jack
So Far Away
It's Too Late
Eventually
Way Over Yonder
Beautiful
You've Got A Friend (w/James Taylor)
Will You Still Love Me Tomorrow
(w/James Taylor)
Some Kind Of Wonderful (w/James Taylor)
Up On The Roof (w/James Taylor)
(You Make Me Feel Like) A Natural Woman

With a guest appearance by then – superstar, James Taylor, Carole King's renowned Carnegie Hall performance was made just that extra bit unique.

George Harrison (& Friends)

Concert For Bangladesh, Madison Square Garden, New York
1st August 1971

Bangla Dhun (Ravi Shankar)
Wah-Wah • My Sweet Lord • Awaiting On You All
(George Harrison & Eric Clapton)
That's The Way God Planned It (Billy Preston)
It Don't Come Easy (Ringo Starr)
Beware Of Darkness (Leon Russell) •
While My Guitar Gently Weeps • Jumpin' Jack
Flash/Young Blood •
Here Comes The Sun (George Harrison) •
A Hard Rain's A-Gonna Fall • It Takes A Lot To
Laugh, It Takes A Train To Cry •
Blowin' In The Wind,
Mr. Tambourine Man • Just Like A Woman (Bob
Dylan & George Harrison) • Something •
Bangladesh (George Harrison)

The original Live Aid. This 'Concert for Bangladesh'
was momentous not only for the appearance of two
Beatles (George and Ringo) on an American stage
for the first time in five years, but also because
George Harrison had persuaded Bob Dylan – who
had rarely performed live since his motorcycle acci-
dent in 1966 – to perform.

Stevie Wonder

Soul Net, New York
1st January 1972

For Once In My Life
If You Really Love Me
Super Woman
You And I
What's Going On
My Cherie Amor
Blowin' In The Wind
With A Child's Heart
Love Having You Around
Signed, Sealed, Delivered, I'm Yours
Papa Was Rolling Stone
Work Out Stevie, Work Out
Superstition
Maybe Your Baby
Superstition 2
Uptight
Intro Jam To Keep On Running
Keep On Running

This gig was performed at a time when Wonder had gained complete artistic control after years as Motown's teenage prodigy. This Soul Net concert was performed shortly before he embarked on a fifty-date tour with The Rolling Stones.

Deep Purple

Budokan, Tokyo, Japan
17th August 1972

Highway Star
Smoke On The Water
Child In Time
Strange Kind Of Woman
Lazy
Space Truckin
Speed King

With the *Guinness Book of Records* having honoured Deep Purple with 'Loudest Band in the World' in 1972, the band set out on this Japanese tour. Thankfully this particular loudness was captured on their 1973 *Made In Japan* album.

Elvis Presley

Honolulu International Center Arena, Honolulu

14th January 1973

See See Rider • Burning Love •
Something • You Gave Me A Mountain •
Steamroller Blues • My Way • Love Me •
Johnny B. Goode • It's Over • Blue Suede Shoes •
I'm So Lonesome I Could Cry •
I Can't Stop Loving You • Hound Dog •
What Now My Love • Fever • Welcome To My
World • Suspicious Minds • I'll Remember You •
Long Tall Sally/Whole Lotta Shakin' Goin' On •
An American Trilogy • A Big Hunk O' Love •
Can't Help Falling In Love

An inspiring vocal with his voice on top form, *Aloha from Hawaii* is yet another legendary Presley performance. The first-ever concert broadcast live via satellite – despite Elvis having secretly taped a fail-safe rehearsal concert the day before. Presley's appearance in a white 'American Eagle' jumpsuit is pretty impressive too, which was helpful, as allegedly one billion people tuned in.

David Bowie

Hang On To Yourself
The Wild Eyed Boy From Freecloud
All the Young Dudes
Oh You Pretty Things
Moonage Daydream
Changes
Space Oddity
Time
Suffragette City
Jean Genie
Love Me Do
Rock 'n' Roll Suicide

Bowie has been responsible for many famous events but none more so than the final night of the *Ziggy Stardust* tour. At the end of this show, Bowie made a speech about this concert being 'the last show we'll ever do' – initiating screams of despair from the audience.

KISS

Coventry Club, Queens, New York
31st December 1973

Deuce
Strutter
She
Firehouse
Nothin' To Lose
100,000 Years
Black Diamond
Let Me Go, Rock And Roll
Cold Gin
Let Me Know

From their very first gig, on this, their first tour, Kiss knew they were going to hit the big time. Powered by industrial amounts of make-up, Kiss emerged as one of the most anthemic, theatrical rock performers of the decade.

Elton John (w/ John Lennon)

Madison Square Garden, New York,
28th November 1974

Funeral For A Friend/Love Lies Bleeding
Rocket Man
Take Me To The Pilot
Bennie And The Jets
Grey Seal
Daniel
You're So Static
Whatever Gets You Through The Night
(w/ John Lennon)
Lucy In The Sky With Diamonds (w/ John Lennon)
I Saw Her Standing There (w/ John Lennon)
Don't Let The Sun Go Down On Me
Your Song
The Bitch Is Back

As a live performer, Elton John very rarely under performs. This was tragically Lennon's last ever live performance.

Talking Heads

CBGB's, New York

8th June 1975

Girls Want To Be With The Girls
Psycho Killer
With Our Love
Artists Only
I Wanna Live
Warning Sign

Despite their Rhode Island roots, the Talking Heads made their debut performance in a tough New York testing ground, supporting none other than the Ramones.

Motörhead

Roundhouse, London
20th July 1975

Motorhead
Leaving Here
Good Morning Little Schoolgirl
Lost Johnny
City Kids
Silver Machine
Waiting For The Man

Motörhead played their first ever show in July 1975.
Their live ferocity was later captured in the awesome *No Sleep 'til Hammersmith*.

Bob Dylan

Madison Square Garden, New York,
8th December 1975

When I Paint My Masterpiece (w/ Bobby
Neuwirth)
It Ain't Me Babe
The Lonesome Death of Hattie Carroll
Tonight I'll Be Staying Here With You
It Takes A Lot to Laugh, It Takes A Train to Cry
(w/ R. Robertson)
Romance In Durango
Isis
The Times They Are A Changin' (w/ Joan Baez)
Dark As A Dungeon (w/ Joan Baez)
Mama You Been On My Mind (w/ Joan Baez)
Never Let Me Go (w/ Joan Baez)
I Dreamed I Saw St. Augustine (w/ Joan Baez)
I Shall Be Released (w/ Joan Baez)
Love Minus Zero/No Limit
Simple Twist of Fate
Oh Sister
Hurricane
One More Cup Of Coffee
Sara
Just Like A Woman
Knockin' On Heaven's Door (w/ Roger McGuinn)
This Land Is Your Land

Dylan's spectacular *Rolling Thunder* tour rolled into
Madison Square Garden – with a few old famous
friends in tow. Dylan closed the show with a Woody
Guthrie song – a personal favourite.

54

Sex Pistols

Lesser Free Trade Hall, Manchester
June 4th 1976

Don't Gimme No Lip Child
I Did You No Wrong
Substitute
No Feelings
Pretty Vacant
Submission
What'cha Gonna Do About It?
No Fun
No Fun

This Sex Pistols performance has been named as one of the most pivotal performances in music history. Members of Joy Division, the Smiths, the Fall and Buzzcocks were in attendance as well as Tony Wilson. Famously, less than 100 people turned up to see the band but, years later, over 1000 swore they were there.

The Clash

100 Club, London
20th September 1976

White Riot
London's Burning
I'm So Bored With The USA
How Can I Understand The Flies
Protex Blue
Deadly Serious
Deny
48 Hours
What's My Name
Janie Jones
1977

As part of the seminal London 100 Club punk all-dayer, this amazing gig boasted a line-up of the Buzzcocks, The Sex Pistols, The Damned and Sid Vicious's first band The Banshees. This gig went down a storm in the tabloid press: not for the line-up mind you, but because an audience member lost an eye.

The Band (& friends)

The Last Waltz, Winterland Ballroom, San Francisco
25th November 1976

Theme From The Last Waltz
(The Band with Orchestra),
Up On Cripple Creek • The Shape I'm In •
It Makes No Difference • Who Do You Love
(The Band with Ronnie Hawkins),
Life Is A Carnival • Such A Night • The Weight •
Down South In New Orleans
(The Band with Dr. John)
This Wheel's On Fire • Mystery Train
(The Band with Paul Butterfield)
Mannish Boy
(The Band with Muddy Waters)
Stagefright • Rag Mama Rag • All Our Past Times
(The Band with Eric Clapton)
Ophelia • Helpless • Four Strong Winds
(The Band with Neil Young)
Coyote • Shadows and Light •
Furry Sings The Blues
(The Band with Joni Mitchell)
Acadian Driftwood
(The Band with Joni Mitchell & Neil Young),
Dry Your Eyes — (The Band with Neil Diamond)
The W.S. Walcott Medicine Show •
Tura Lura Lura • Caravan
(The Band with Van Morrison)
The Night They Drove Old Dixie Down •

57

The Genetic Method/Chest Fever • Baby, Let Me
Follow You Down • Hazel • I Don't Believe You
(She Acts Like We Never Have Met) •
Forever Young • Baby, I Shall Be Released
(The Band with Bob Dylan),
Don't Do It • Greensleves • The Well •
Evangeline
(The Band with Emmylou Harris),
Out Of The Blue • The Weight
(The Band with Maris & Roebuck Staples),
The Last Waltz Refrain • Theme From The Last
Waltz • King Harvest (Has Surely Come),
Rag Mama Rag • Mad Waltz
(sketch track for 'The Well'),
The Last Waltz Theme
(Robbie Robertson)

After sixteen years of touring, The Band finally
decided to disband. Martin Scorcese, always with a
keen eye, wanted to celebrate the last hurrah of
America's greatest group by filming it. The
Winterland Ballroom was chosen as it was the first
venue the group played under the name 'The Band'.
Bizarrely, the Sex Pistols would play their last show
here just over a year later.

Sex Pistols

Anarchy In The UK
I Wanna Be Me
Seventeen
Stepping Stone
God Save The Queen
Substitute
No Feelings
Liar
Pretty Vacant
Problems
Whatcha Gonna Do About It?
No Fun

As the opening night of the blighted *Anarchy In The UK* Tour (with the Clash, Johnny Thunders & the Heartbreakers and The Damned), the Pistols kick-started the show off with a vitriolic thrashing of 'Anarchy in the UK'. The audience was stunned. The disaffected youth stood in awe. Other bands took note.

The Clash

Guildford Civic Hall, Surrey

1st May 1977

London's Burning
1977
I'm So Bored With The USA
Pressure Drop
Hate And War
Cheat
Police And Thieves
48 Hours
Capital Radio
Deny
Remote Control
Career Opportunities
White Riot
Janie Jones
Garageland
1977

This show was part of their first ever full-scale tour, not taking into consideration the 1976 *Anarchy In The UK Tour* supporting the Sex Pistols, of which all but three shows were shambolically cancelled.

The Eagles

Hotel California
Lyin' Eyes
Wasted Time
Take It To The Limit
Desperado
Midnight Flyer
Turn To Stone
Already Gone
One Of These Nights
Funk #49
Good Day In Hell
Rocky Mountain Way
Witchy Woman
James Dean
The Best of My Love
Walk Away
Tequila Sunrise

Once Linda Ronstadt's backing group, The Eagles, at the time of this show, were the biggest band in the world touring what later would become one of the most popular albums of all time. Founding member Randy Meisner, quit shortly after this *Hotel California* tour.

AC/DC

Hammersmith Odeon, London

25th October 1977

Let There Be Rock
Problem Child
Whole Lotta Rosie
Hell Ain´t A Bad Place To Be
High Voltage
She's Got The Jack
Bad Boy Boogie
I'm A Rocker

Neatly coinciding with punk's late '70s rasp,
AC/DC made their mark as a live act, with a heavier
sound and a more theatrical stage show, in which
manic Angus wore a school uniform. A premature
tour to promote *Let There Be Rock* (1977) began
badly, with half empty venues, but one such show
was the turning point, with a now legendary setlist,
featuring 'Whole Lotta Rosie' and a breakneck
version of 'I'm a Rocker'.

Iggy Pop

Civic Auditorium, Santa Monica
18th November 1977

Raw Power
TV Eye
Dirt
1969
Turn Blue
Funtime
Gimme Danger
No Fun
Sister Midnight
I Need Somebody
Search & Destroy
I Wanna Be Your Dog
Lust For Life
The Passenger
Nightclubbing
One Two Brown Eyes

After years of a rock 'n' roll lifestyle taken to the extreme, Iggy Pop decided '77 was the year to sort himself out. He checked into a mental institution, while David Bowie not only nurtured him back to health, but contributed to Iggy's most successful year after producing both *The Idiot* and *Lust For Life*. This gig certified his comeback, in true Pop style.

Sex Pistols

Winterland Ballroom, San Francisco,
14th January 1978

God Save The Queen
I Wanna Be Me
17
New York
E.M.I.
Belson Was A Gas
Bodies
Holidays In The Sun
Liar
No Feelings
Problems
Pretty Vacant
Anarchy In The U.S.A.
No Fun

The Pistol's last gig ever (before the *Filthy Lucre* reunion tour of 1996) was typically chaotic. 'Ever get the feeling you've been cheated?' Johnny Rotten sneered to the audience before throwing down his microphone and walking off stage.

Bob Marley & The Wailers

Lion Of Judah
Natural Mystic
Trenchtown Rock
Natty Dread
Positive Vibration
War
Jammin'
One Love/People Get Ready
Jah Live

This was Marley's first show in Jamaica after the earlier attempt on his life in December 1976. All of the original Wailers reunited for the gig and during 'Jammin', Marley called up Prime Minister Michael Manley and the opposition party leader, Edward Seaga, to join hands. After a few anxious moments, they did and together with Bob sang 'One Love'.

Bruce Springsteen

The Roxy, Los Angeles
7th July 1978

Rave On • Badlands • Spirit In The night •
Darkness On The Edge Of Town • Candy's
Room • For You • Point Blank • The Promised
Land • Prove It All Night • Racing In The Street •
Thunder Road • Paradise By The C • Fire •
Adam Raised A Cain • Mona • She's The One •
Growin' Up • It's Hard To Be A Saint In the City
• Backstreets • Sad Eyes • Heartbreak Hotel •
Rosalita • Independence Day • Born To Run •
Because The Night • Raise Your Hand •
Twist And Shout

Voted as one of the best shows The Boss has ever
played, this *Darkness On the Edge Of Town* tour is
often hailed as one of the greatest rock and roll tours
of all time too.

Neil Young (w/ Crazy Horse)

The Forum, Los Angeles, CA
23rd October 1978

Sugar Mountain
I Am A Child
Comes A Time
Already One
After The Goldrush
My My, Hey Hey (Out Of the Blue)
When You Dance I Can Really Love
The Loner
Welfare Mothers
Come On Baby Let's Go Downtown
Needle & The Damage Done
Lotta Love
Sedan Delivery
Powderfinger
Cortez The Killer
Cinnamon Girl
Like A Hurricane
Hey Hey, My My
Tonight's The Night

This *Rust Never Sleeps* set tipified Young's mammoth
world tour of 1978, when Crazy Horse played in
front of giant Marshall stacks and roadies dressed as
Star Wars aliens.

Parliament

Convention Center, Dallas

5th November 1976

Cosmic Slop
Let's Take It To The Stage
Do That Stuff
Standing On The Verge Of Getting It On
The Undisco Kidd
Mothership Connection
Swing Down, Sweet Chariot
Dr. Funkenstein
Comin' 'Round The Mountain
Give Up The Funk
Night Of The Thumpasaurus Peoples
We Want The Funk/Funkin' For Fun
Parliament Funkadelic

As reserved as their song titles, Parliament were a
mind-boggling live extravaganza in the mid 1970s.
This Texas show, as part of their *Mothership Tour*,
featured George Clinton (wearing an eye-popping
costume) inside a giant spaceship that 'landed'
onstage.

Led Zeppelin

Knebworth Festival, Stevenage
11th August 1979

The Song Remains The Same/Celebration Day
Black Dog
Nobody's Fault But Mine
Over The Hills And Far Away
Misty Mountain Hop
Since I've Been Loving You
No Quarter
Hot Dog
The Rain Song
White Summer/Black Mountain Side/Kashmir
Trampled Underfoot
Sick Again
Achilles Last Stand
In The Evening
Stairway To Heaven
Rock And Roll
Whole Lotta Love
Communication Breakdown

With complaints from over six miles away about the noise, it soon became evident that Led Zeppelin had returned. Amid rumours of a split in 1978 – and a few years recovering from personal tragedies – the band made a dramatic re-appearance at the famous Knebworth.

The Clash

The Palladium, New York
21st September 1979

Safe European Home
I'm So Bored With The USA
Complete Control
London Calling
White Man In Hammersmith Palais
Koka-Kola
I Fought The Law
Jail Guitar Doors
The Guns Of Brixton
English Civil War
Clash City Rockers
Stay Free
Clampdown
Police And Thieves
Capital Radio One
Tommy Gun
Wrong 'Em Boyo
Janie Jones
Garageland
Armagideon Time
Career Opportunities
What's My Name
White Riot

The image that adorns the famous cover of *London Calling* was taken at this New York Palladium gig. The iconic photograph of bassist Paul Simonon smashing his malfunctioning bass was taken by rock photographer Pennie Smith. This was Simonon's only time he took his frustrations out on a guitar on stage. He still has the pieces.

Abba

Voulez-Vous
Knowing Me Knowing You
Chiquita
Gimme, Gimme
Super Trooper
I Have A Dream
Thank You For The Music
2 For The Price Of 1
Fernando
Take A Chance On Me
Does Your Mother Know
Hole In Your Soul
Money, Money
Old Friends
On & On & On
Waterloo
Dancing Queen

Abba. A sold out Wembley Stadium. The Seventies.
What's not to love?

The Police

Orpheum Theatre, Boston
27th November 1979

Next To You
So Lonely
Truth Hits Everybody
Walking On The Moon
Hole In My Life
Fall Out
Bring On The Night
Message In A Bottle
The Bed's Too Big Without You
Peanuts
Roxanne
Can't Stand Losing You
Landlord
Born In The 50's
Be My Girl (Sally)

Sting and Stewart Copeland's differing personalities (and egos) always made for energetic, sometimes tense, performances. This particular concert was so good it was later released as their *Live* album in 1995.

Joy Division

Birmingham University, Birmingham
2nd May 1980

Ceremony
Shadow Play
Means To An End
Passover
New Dawn Fades
Transmission
7
Disorder
Isolation
Decades
Digital

This was, sadly, the band's last ever gig. Ian Curtis, the band's troubled leader, stumbled offstage during ' Decades'. The band played on without him. Curtis reappeared for the final song not knowing it would be the last time they would play live together.

The Blues Brothers

Universal Amphitheater, Los Angeles
1st August 1980

Soul Finger/Everybody Needs Somebody To Love
Hey Bartender
She Caught The Katy And Left Me A Mule To Ride
Messin' With The Kid
Expressway To Your Heart
I Ain't Got You
Rubber Biscuit
Shotgun Blues
Almost
Do You Love Me
B Movie Box Car Blues
Green Onions
Going Back To Miami
Gimmie Some Lovin'
Come On Up
I Don't Know
From The Bottom
Who's Making Love
Guilty
Perry Mason Theme / Riot In Cell Block Number Nine
Jailhouse Rock
Flip, Flop & Fly
Theme From 'Rawhide'
Soul Man/I Can't Turn You Loose

The Blues Brothers were a rare phenomemen – two white American comedians (John Belushi and Dan Akyroyd) paying tribute to the soul, blues and R 'n' B that ingrained itself in American culture. This was the last Blues Brothers show before John Belushi's death.

Ray Charles

Northern Alberta Jubilee Auditorium, Edmonton
27th January 1981

Riding Thumb
Busted
Georgia On My Mind
Oh, What A Beautiful Morning
Some Enchanted Evening
Hit The Road Jack
I Can't Stop Loving You
Take These Chains From My Heart
I Can See Clearly Now
What'd I Say
America The Beautiful

This Edmonton show was spectacular even by Ray Charles' standards. Recorded live for television, the set featured Charles's rousing version of 'Hit the Road Jack' through to the classic 'What'd I Say'.

Pink Floyd

Earls Court, London
17th June 1981

In The Flesh • The Thin Ice •
Another Brick In The Wall I •
The Happiest Days Of Our Lives •
Another Brick In The Wall II • Mother •
Goodbye Blue Sky • What Shall We Do Now? •
Young Lust • One Of My Turns •
Don't Leave Me Now • Another Brick In The
Wall III • Goodbye Cruel World • Hey You •
Is There Anybody Out There? • Nobody Home •
Vera • Bring The Boys Back Home •
Comfortably Numb • The Show Must Go On •
In The Flesh? • Run Like Hell •
Waiting For The Worms • Stop • The Trial •
Outside The Wall

Performed in only a few cities due its grandiose
design and setting, *The Wall* show is one of the most
visually and sonically stunning stage set pieces ever
presented. This show was the band's live swansong
before reforming for Live8 in 2005.

Simon and Garfunkel

Central Park, New York
19th September 1981

Mrs Robinson
Homeward Bound
America
Me And Julio Down By The Schoolyard
Scarborough Fair
April Come She Will
Wake Up Little Suzie
Still Crazy After All These Years
American Tune
Late In The Evening
Slip Sliding Away
A Heart In New York
The Late Great Johnny Ace
Kodachrome
Maybellene
Bridge Over Troubled Water
Fifty Ways To Leave Your Lover
The Boxer
Old Friends
Feeling Groovy
The Sound of Silence
Late in the Evening

After splitting in 1970, and Simon's subsequent solo
career, the pair reunited for a free concert in Central
Park. Over 500,000 people turned up.

Ozzy Osbourne

Veteran's Memorial Auditorium, Des Moines
20th January 1982

Over The Mountain
Mr. Crowley
Crazy Train
Revelation (Mother Earth)
Steal Away (The Night)
Suicide Solution
Goodbye To Romance
I Don't Know
No Bone Movies
Believer
Flying High Again
Iron Man
Children Of The Grave
Paranoid

The bat biting gig. During the set, which consisted of Sabbath and solo Ozzy material, a fan tossed a dead bat onto the stage. Ozzy, thinking it was a rubber bat, bit its head off. He was given a rabies injection promptly after the show.

The Jam

Start!
It's Too Bad
Beat Surrender
Away From The Numbers
Ghosts
In The Crowd
Boy About Town
Get Yourself Together
All Mod Cons/To Be Someone
Smithers-Jones
Tales From The Riverbank
Precious
Move On Up
Circus
Down In The Tube Station At Midnight
David Watts
Mr. Clean
Going Underground
In The City
Town Called Malice
The Butterfly Collector
Pretty Green
The Gift

This Brighton show, their final performance together, ended a lengthy and emotional farewell tour with Paul Weller having announced to Bruce Foxton and Rick Buckler that he was leaving six months previously.

U2

Red Rocks Amphitheatre, Morrison, Colorado
5th June 1983

Out Of Control
Twilight
An Cat Dubh
Into The Heart
Surrender
Two Hearts Beat As One
Seconds
Sunday Bloody Sunday
The Cry / The Electric Co.
I Fall Down
October
New Year's Day
I Threw A Brick Through A Window
A Day Without Me
Gloria
Party Girl
11 O' Clock Tick Tock
I Will Follow
40

Playing to 9000 fans, this was a momentous time for U2 and the band's decision to record this gig was later included in *Rolling Stone*'s list of the '50 Moments that Changed Rock and Roll'.

The Smiths

Free Trade Hall, Manchester
13th March 1984

Hand In Glove
Heaven Knows I'm Miserable Now
Girl Afraid
This Charming Man
Pretty Girls Make Graves
Still Ill
This Night Has Opened My Eyes
Barbarism Begins At Home
Back To The Old House
What Difference Does It Make?
I Don't Owe You Anything (w/ Sandie Shaw)
Reel Around The Fountain
You've Got Everything Now
Handsome Devil
These Things Take Time

One of the earliest gigs from The Smiths' first major UK tour in support of their debut album. The band's fans were rowdier than the venue's security staff were expecting. The first four rows of the stalls completely collapsed as the audience jumped on the backs of the seats, causing a panic.

Status Quo

Milton Keynes Bowl

21st July 1984

Caroline
Roll Over Lay Down
Whatever You Want
Mystery Song/Railroad/Most Of The Time/Wild
Side Of Life/Slow Train
Rockin' All Over The World
Dirty Water
Roadhouse Blues
What You're Proposing
Down Down
Bye Bye Johnny

This concert was supposed to be Quo's big retirement gig – a whopping 125,000 fans turned up to say farewell. The band cited 'enough was enough'. It didn't last long though, and they were back together in no time.

Prince

Controversy • Let's Go Crazy •
Delirious • 1999 • Little Red Corvette •
Take Me With U •
When You Were Mine •
4 The Tears In Your Eyes •
Yankee Doodle Dandy • A Case Of You • Free •
Raspberry Beret • Do Me, Baby •
Irresistible Bitch • Temptation •
Let's Pretend We're Married •
International Lover • Conversation • God •
Computer Blue • Darling Nikky •
The Beautiful Ones • When Doves Cry •
I Would Die 4 U • Baby, I'm A Star
(w/ Madonna & Bruce Springsteen) • America •
Purple Rain • 4 The Tears In Your Eyes

At the height of his fame, Prince's eccentric lifestyle was under scrutiny, and one of the most electric live performers decided to temporarily retire from the stage. His reason? To 'look for the ladder'.

Queen

Live Aid, Wembley Stadium, London
13th July 1985

Bohemian Rhapsody
Radio Ga Ga
Hammer To Fall
Crazy Little Thing Called Love
We Will Rock You
We Are The Champions

In a line up of many of the world's greatest stars, Queen's performance at Live Aid stole the show. In 2005, this six song set was voted as the world's greatest ever rock gig. Not bad for twenty minutes work.

Guns N' Roses

Reckless Life
Out Ta Get Me
Welcome To The Jungle
Jumpin' Jack Flash
Think About You
Move To The City
Rocket Queen
Nightrain
Back Off Bitch
Anything Goes

Despite only 20 people turning up at their first ever gig, the band soon earned a residency at this L.A. nightspot – and quickly became one of the hottest groups on the rock scene.

Jean Michel Jarre

Houston, Texas
5th April 1986

Ethnicolor part 1
Oxygene Part 1
Oxygene Part 2
Oxygene Part 4
Equinoxe Part 7
Souvenir of China
Equinoxe Part4
Equinoxe Part
Equinoxe Part 5
Rendez-Vous 3
Rendez-Vous 2
Oxygene Part 5
Rendez-Vous 6
Rendez-Vous 4

Attracting over 1.5 million people, Jean Michel
Jarre's Houston performance gained entry into the
Guinness Book of Records for the largest audience ever
for an outdoor show. In celebration of NASA's 25th
Anniversary, gigantic images and lasers were
projected onto downtown Houston's skyscrapers
causing freeways to be closed down.

The Smiths

Brixton Academy, London
12th December 1986

Ask
Bigmouth Strikes Again
London
Miserable Lie
Some Girls Are Bigger Than Others
The Boy With The Thorn In His Side
Shoplifters Of The World Unite
There Is A Light That Never Goes Out
Is It Really So Strange?
Cemetary Gates
This Night Has Opened My Eyes
Still Ill
Panic
The Queen Is Dead
William It Was Really Nothing
Hand In Glove

By 1986 Morrissey and Marr's relationship was in devestating meltdown and after five years together as The Smiths the group completely self-destructed. This was their final gig.

Public Enemy

Greek Theater, Los Angeles
27th June 1988

Don't Believe The Hype
Cold Lampin With Flav
Rebel Without A Pause
Terminator X To The Edge Of Panic
Bring The Noise
Prophet's Of Rage
Hazy Shade Of Criminal

Two months after the release of the group's mag-
num opus, *It Takes A Nation Of Millions To Hold
Us Back*, the New York rappers performed on
the West Coast. On the evidence of this gig, the
audience *did* believe the hype.

The Beastie Boys

Slow And Low
It's The New Style
She's Crafty
Time To Get Ill
Paul Revere
Rhymin' And Stealin'
Posse In Effect
She's On It
Brass Monkey
Hold It Now Hit It!
No Sleep Till Brooklyn
(You Gotta) Fight For Your Right To Party

The year, you could argue, hip hop arrived onto Britain's shores. The Beastie Boys came in support of hip hop giants Run DMC: No Volkswagen was safe.

Roy Orbison

Coconut Grove, Los Angeles
30th September 1987

Only The Lonely
Dream Baby (How Long Must I Dream)
Blue Bayou
The Comedians
Ooby Dooby
Leah
Running Scared
Uptown
In Dreams
Crying
Candyman
Go, Go, Go (Down The Line)
Mean Woman Blues
(All I Can Do Is) Dream You
Claudette
It's Over
Oh, Pretty Woman

The 'Big O' orchestrated this concert in 1987 after his induction into the Rock and Roll Hall of Fame. Performed in the now-flattened Coconut Grove his stage band included Jackson Browne, Elvis Costello, Bonnie Raitt, Bruce Springsteen and Tom Waits, along with the rhythm section from Elvis Presley's touring band, the Jordannaires.

Michael Jackson

Wembley Stadium, London
14th July 1988

Wanna Be Startin' Somethin'
Things I Do For You
Off The Wall
Human Nature
Heartbreak Hotel
She's Out Of My Life
I Want You Back/The Love You Save/I'll Be There
Rock With You
You Are My Lovely One
Working Day And Night
Beat It
Billie Jean
Shake Your Body (Down To The Ground)
Thriller
I Just Can't Stop Loving You
Bad

Michael Jackson's first ever solo tour. An enormous 504,000 people turned up for his seven night sell-out run at Wembley earning him another entry in *The Guinness Book Of World Records*.

David Hasselhoff

Berlin Wall, Germany

31st January 1989

Looking For Freedom

After two moderately successful albums, the Hoff became an unlikely, but incredibly successful, German superstar. This track, with its 'poetic' lyrics, seemed to resonate with the newly unified nation and so he performed it on top of the Wall on New Year's Eve, 1989.

R.E.M.

Macon County Coliseum, Macon, Georgia
11th November 1989

Stand • The One I Love • So. Central Rain •
Turn You Inside-Out • Belong •
Exhuming McCarthy • Good Advices •
Orange Crush • Feeling Gravity's Pull •
Time After Time (Annelise) • These Days •
World Leader Pretend • Future 40s - I Believe •
Eleventh Untitled Song • Get Up •
Auctioneer (Another Engine) •
It's The End Of The World As We Know It (And
I Feel Fine) • Pop Song 89 • Fall On Me •
You Are The Everything • Harpers •
Begin The Begin • King Of Birds • See No Evil •
Low • Finest Worksong • Perfect Circle •
Dark Globe • After Hours

R.E.M.'s final show of their breakthrough *Green*
world tour. It was a homecoming show for the
Atlanta foursome who – amazingly judging from
this setlist – had yet to release their biggest
international hit.

Happy Mondays

G-Mex Arena, Manchester
15th March 1990

Rave On
Do It Better
Tart Tart
Step On
Performance
Hallelujah
Clap Your Hands
Kuff Dam
Lazyitis
24 Hour Party People
Mad Cyril
Gods Cop
Wrote For Luck

This hometown show, at the band's peak, was euphoric. But then it could have been the drugs.

The Stone Roses

Spike Island, Widnes,
27th May 1990

I Wanna Be Adored
Elephant Stone
She Bangs The Drums
Shoot You Down
One Love
Sally Cinnamon
(Song For My) Sugar Spun Sister
Standing Here
Fools Gold
Where Angels Play
Waterfall
Don't Stop
Something's Burning
Made Of Stone
Elizabeth My Dear

In 1990 the Stone Roses sounded like a band that were changing the world. This Spike Island gig has become the defining moment of their early success.

The Cure

Glastonbury Festival, Pilton, Somerset
23rd June 1990

Shake Dog Shake
A Strange Day
A Night Like This
Just Like Heaven
The Walk
Primary
In-between Days
A Forest
Disintegration
Close To Me
Let's Go To Bed
Why Can't I Be You?
Lulllaby
Lament
10:15 Saturday Night
Killing An Arab
Never Enough
Boys Don't Cry (Unplugged)

The 1990 festival took the name of the Glastonbury Festival for Contemporary Performing Arts for the first time, to reflect the diversity of attractions within it. One of those attractions being The Cure, fresh from success in the US. Incidentally, Robert Smith made reference to the fact that they only play Glastonbury when the World Cup is being played.

Madonna

Stadio Flaminio, Rome
10th July 1990

Express Yourself
Open Your Heart
Causing A Commotion
Where's The Party
Like A Virgin
Like A Prayer
Live To Tell/Oh Father
Papa Don't Preach
Sooner Or Later
Hanky Panky
Now I'm Following You Part 1 & 2
Material Girl
Cherish
Into The Groove
Vogue
Holiday
Family Affair/Keep It Together

Jean Paul Gaultier's cone brassiere aside, Madonna's *Blonde Ambition* tour of 1990 is considered to have changed the world of pop concerts forever. On this tour, The Pope called for Madonna's Italian shows, three in total, to be cancelled. Only one was.

Aerosmith

Monsters Of Rock Festival, Castle Donington
18th August 1990

Young Lust
F.I.N.E.
Monkey On My Back
Janie's Got A Gun
Rag Doll
Voodoo Medicine Man
Love In An Elevator
Dude (Looks Like A Lady)
Sweet Emotion
Toys In The Attic
Dream On
Train Kept A Rollin' (w/ Jimmy Page)
Walk This Way (w/ Jimmy Page)

A great show from one of the great rock bands. For everyone who remembers being at this gig (the band surely don't) we know that it was one worth remembering.

98

Bingo Hand Job

World Leader Pretend • Half A World Away •
Fretless • The One I Love (R.E.M.) • Cindy Of A
Thousand Lives • The Old Triangle • Reason To
Believe • Hello In There • My Youngest Son
Came Home Today (Billy Bragg solo) • Jackson •
Dallas • Disturbance at the Heron House •
Belong • Low • Love Is All Around (R.E.M.) •
Come Dance With Me • Lonely Is As Lonely
Does (Peter Holsapple solo) • Neverland • Wire
Train (Peter Holsapple solo) • You Are the
Everything • Swan Swan H • Radio Song • Perfect
Circle • Oceanside • Ultra-Unbelievable Love •
Birdshead • Queen of Eyes (Robyn Hitchcock
solo) • Endgame • Pop Song 89 (Michael Stipe
solo) • Losing My Religion • Fall On Me (Michael
Stipe solo) • Tom's Diner • Listening to the
Higsons • You Ain't Goin' Nowhere (ensemble) •
Get Up • Moon River (R.E.M.)

Played over a series of three nights and under the
wonderfully titillating pseudonym 'Bingo Hand
Job', R.E.M.'s UK showcasing of *Out of Time* was
extraordinary. With Billy Bragg, Robyn Hitchcock
and Peter Holsapple joining in for the fun this is
regarded as one of R.E.M's finest shows.

U2

Lakeland Arena, Lakeland, Florida
29th February 1992

Zoo Station
The Fly
Even Better Than The Real Thing
Mysterious Ways
One
Until The End Of The World
Who's Gonna Ride Your Wild Horses
Trying To Throw Your Arms Around The World
Angel Of Harlem
Satellite Of Love
Bad/All I Want Is You
Bullet The Blue Sky
Running To Stand Still
Where The Streets Have No Name
Pride (In The Name Of Love)
I Still Haven't Found What I'm Looking For
Desire
Ultraviolet (Light My Way)
With Or Without You
Love Is Blindness

Differing wildly from any U2 show before it, this first gig of the *Zoo TV* tour has been called the 'most spectacular rock show every staged by a band'. With use of slogans, visual effects and news reports this show was the first of a kind, ushering in the age of concerts as 'multimedia' events.

Jeff Buckley

Lover You Should Have Come Over
Dream Brother
Eternal Life
Kick Out The Jams
Lilac Wine
Grace
That's All I Ask
Kashmir
Je N'en Connais Pas La Fin
Hallelujah
What Will You Say

Playing at the venue made famous by Edith Piaf,
Buckley felt at ease and comfortable in a venue with
so much history. Buckley later claimed it was the
finest performance of his unfortunately brief career.

Oasis

The Boardwalk, Manchester
1st January 1992

Columbia
Take Me
Must Be The Music
Acoustic Song
I Will Show You
Better Let You Know
Poetic Feedback

Oasis's first gig as Oasis. Before Noel joined The Rain, as they were originally known, the band lacked the songwriting clout that Liam's older brother had in spades. Only a few of these songs creeped into future setlists but this gig is proof the band had a vicious sound even from these early live shows.

Nirvana

Reading Festival, Reading
30th August 1992

The Rose • Breed • Drain You • Aneurysm •
School • Sliver • In Bloom • Come As You Are •
Lithium • About A Girl • Tourettes • Polly •
Lounge Act • More Than A Feeling Jam •
Smells Like Teen Spirit • On A Plain •
Negative Creep • Been A Son • All Apologies •
Blew • Dumb • Stay Away • Spank Thru •
Love Buzz • The Money Will Roll Right In • D-7 •
Territorial Pissings • Star Spangled Banner

A triumphant show and widely acknowledged as
one of the most electrifying gigs of the last twenty
years – even the band themselves citing it as their
favourite gig. Their last ever UK appearance.

Red Hot Chilli Peppers

Lollapalooza, New Orleans
4th September 1992

Suck My Kiss
Subterranean Homesick Blues
My Lovely Man
Nobody Weird Like Me
If You Have To Ask
Stone Cold Bush
Blood Sugar Sex Magic
Higher Ground
Magic Johnson
Under The Bridge
I Wanna Party On Your Pussy
The Needle And The Damage Done
Me And My Friends
Mommy, Where's Daddy?
Crosstown Traffic

Labelled the 'Woodstock of the '90s', Lollapalooza was the US's biggest American alternative music festival. As headline act, this was also the first time the Pepper's included new guitarist Arik Marshall after John Frusciante needed to 'take a break'.

Oasis

King Tut's Wah Wah, Glasgow
31st May 1993

Rock 'n' Roll Star
Up In The Sky
Bring It On Down
I Am The Walrus

Having travelled up to Glasgow that day, Oasis barged onto the bill by threatening the club's bouncers to let them play or risk the band trashing the place. They were the first band on and with only a small audience watching managed to grab the attention of Creation Records boss Alan McGee. He signed them up there and then.

Nirvana
MTV Unplugged, Sony Music Studios, New York
18th November 1993

About A Girl
Come As You Are
Jesus Doesn't Want Me For A Sunbeam
The Man Who Sold The World
Pennyroyal Tea
Dumb
Polly
On A Plain
Something In The Way
Plateau
Oh, Me
Lake Of Fire
All Apologies
Where Did You Sleep Last Night

One of the last televised performances by Kurt Cobain, recorded just a few months before his death. Raw and beautiful, it was hailed by critics as proof Nirvana were able to transcend the angst-ridden 'grunge' tag.

Nirvana

Palatrussardi, Milan, Italy
25th February 1994

Radio Friendly Unit Shifter
Drain You
Breed
Serve The Servants
Come As You Are
Smells Like Teen Spirit
Sliver
Dumb
In Bloom
About A Girl
Lithium
Pennyroyal Tea
School
Polly
Francis Farmer
Verse Chorus Verse
Rape Me
Territorial Pissings
All Apologies
On A Plain
Scentless Apprentice
Heart Shaped Box

Nirvana's last ever gig. With touring guitarist Pat Smear in place, the band's sound was getting bigger and better, making Kurt's death all the more tragic.

Blur

Mile End, London
17th June 1995

Tracy Jacks
Sunday, Sunday
Chemical World
End Of A Century
She's So High
Globe Alone
Country House
Jubilee
Badhead
Girls & Boys
Stereotypes
Far Out
Bank Holiday
For Tomorrow
Parklife
Daisy Bell (A Bicycle Built For Two)
This Is A Low

On June 17, 1995, Blur played their first stadium concert and it was a defining highlight in a year obsessed with Britpop. Later on, it would all be about the battle with Oasis, but here it was very much Blur's moment.

Pulp

Glastonbury Festival, Pilton, Somerset
24th June 1995

Do You Remember The First Time
Razzamatazz
Monday Morning
Underwear
Sorted For E's And Wizz
Disco 2000
Joyriders
Acrylic Afternoons
Mis-shapes
Pink Glove
Babies
Common People

Filling in for the Stone Roses' Saturday night headline slot when guitarist John Squire broke his collar bone (on what was meant to be a UK comeback for them) Pulp stepped up to the challenge and performed a career-making show.

Foo Fighters

Reading Festival, Reading
26th August 1995

Winnebago
I'll Stick Around
Butterflies
Wattershed
Big Me
This Is A Call
Weenie Beenie
For All The Cows
Oh, George
Podunk
Good Grief
Alone And Easy Target
X-Static
My Hero
Exhausted

Dave Grohl's first major live outing with a new band after Kurt Cobain's suicide, and the end of Nirvana, in 1994. Playing the relatively small BBC Radio One tent almost 15,000 people tried to cram in. The band had to stop songs throughout the show and help people out of the crowd who had fainted.

Oasis

Maine Road, Manchester
27th April 1996

The Swamp Song
Acquiesce
Supersonic
Hello
Some Might Say
Roll With It
Morning Glory
Round Are Way
Cigarettes & Alcohol
Champagne Supernova
Cast No Shadow
Wonderwall
The Masterplan
Don t Look Back In Anger
Live Forever
I Am The Walrus
Cum On Feel The Noize

Oasis played to 80,000 fans over two nights at the home of the Gallagher Brother's favourite football club. For once a stunning home performance at Maine Road.

Oasis

Knebworth Park Knebworth
10th August 1996

Swamp Song
Columbia
Acquiesce
Supersonic
Hello
Some Might Say
Slide Away
Roll With It
Morning Glory
Round Are Way
Cigarettes & Alcohol
Whatever
Cast No Shadow
Wonderwall
The Masterplan
Don't Look Back In Anger
My Big Mouth
It's Getting Better, Man
Live Forever
Champagne Supernova (w/ John Squire)
I Am The Walrus

'This is history!' Noel Gallagher exclaimed walking out onto the stage in front of 250,000 people. 'No, its not yer fucking daft twat. This is Knebworth' Liam Gallagher followed. Oasis's record-breaking two-night stand was the definitive high point of the 1990s UK music scene.

Stone Roses

Reading Festival, Reading
25th August 1996

She Bangs The Drums
Waterfall
High Time
Ten Storey Love Song
Daybreak
Love Spreads
Made Of Stone
I Am The Resurrection
Ice Cold Cube
Breaking Into Heaven

The Stone Roses' shambolic and tuneless demise just so happened to be in front of a bemused 60,000 festival-goers. The band had stumbled on, though guitarist John Squire and drummer Reni now having been replaced by Aziz Abrahim and Robbie Maddix. The classic 'Fools Gold' is notable in the set by its absence. Apparently, Maddix was unable to emulate Reni's original rhythm.

Radiohead

Glastonbury Festival, Pilton, Somerset
28th June 1997

Lucky
My Iron Lung
Airbag
Planet Telex
Exit Music (For A Film)
The Bends
Nice Dream
Paranoid Android
Karma Police
Creep
Climbing Up The Walls
No Surprises
Talk Show Host
Bones
Just
Fake Plastic Trees
You
The Tourist
High & Dry
Street Spirit (Fade Out)

Radiohead's first gig since the release of *OK Computer* a few days earlier was going to attract much attention. However, this performance is considered by many, including the festival's founder Michael Eavis, as the finest performance in the history of the event – despite the torrential 'soup' of mud and rain.

Prodigy

Smack My Bitch Up
Voodoo People
Breathe
Poison
Funky Shit
Their Law
Fire Drill
Serial Thrilla
Mindfields
Rock 'n' Roll
Firestarter
Full Throttle

With a mix of the old and new stuff, both equally electrifying, the Prodigy did not fail too disappoint the hungry crowd. The band, renowned for never returning for an encore, famously re-emerged after the set was over. That's just how good it was.

Paul McCartney

The Cavern, Liverpool
14th December 1999

Honey Hush
Blue Jean Pop
Brown-eyed Handsome Man
Fabulous
What Is It
Lonesome Town
Twenty Flight Rock
No Other Baby
Try Not To Cry
Shake A Hand
All Shook Up
Party

The show – McCartney's first at the tiny, historic venue since The Beatles last played there on August 3rd, 1963 – was, unbelievably, his 281st show at The Cavern.

Pearl Jam

Roskilde Festival, Denmark
30th June 2000

Animal
Better Man
Breaker Fall
Corduroy
Daughter
Even Flow
Given To Fly
Habit
Hail, Hail
Insignificance
Light Years
MFC

Perhaps remembered for all the wrong reasons, this Pearl Jam gig ended in tragedy. Before the band realized what was happening, nine people were crushed to death under the movement of fans rushing to the front of the stage to mosh.

U2

Elevation
Beautiful Day
Until The End Of The World
New Year's Day
Out Of Control
Sunday Bloody Sunday
Wake Up Dead Man
Stuck In A Moment You Can't Get Out Of
Kite
Angel Of Harlem
Desire
Staring At The Sun
All I Want Is You
Where The Streets Have No Name
Pride (In The Name Of Love)
Bullet the Blue Sky
With Or Without You
One
Walk On

Having 're-applied for biggest band in the world' U2 returned home to where they recorded their breakout album *The Unforgettable Fire*. Tragically, Bono's father had died a week before this show, making it all the more poignant for the singer. 'Kite' was in his honour and a tearful Bono struggled to get through the song.

Eminem

Ford Field, Detroit

12th July 2003

Square Dance
Business
White America
Kill You
When The Music Stops
Pimp Like Me
Fight Music
Purple Pills
Stan
Way I Am
Soldier
Cleaning Out My Closet
Drips
Run Rabbit Run
Love Me
Wanksta
In Da Club
21 Questions
Patiently Waiting
Lose Yourself
8 Mile
Superman
Drug Ballad
Sing For The Moment
Without Me
Dad's Gone Crazy
Rap Game

Eminem's triumphant show in the Motor City to 95,000 fans has been deemed 'the grandest hip-hop spectacle ever.' With opening sets from 50 Cent and Missy Elliott (plus appearances by Proof, D-12 and Obie Trice) this homecoming gig put Detroit back on the musical map.

Robbie Williams

Knebworth Park Knebworth
2nd August 2003

Let Me Entertain Me
Let Love Be Your Energy
We Will Rock You
Monsoon
Come Undone
Strong
Me And My Monkey
Hot Fudge
Mr. Bojangles
She's The One
Supreme
No Regrets
Kids
Better Man
Nan's Song
Feel
Rock DJ
Angels
Back For Good

Beating Oasis's two-night stay in 1996 with an extra night, Robbie Williams proved his dominance of the British pop scene. Playing to 375,000 fans over three nights, Robbie may have tripped up on stage mid-set to the amusement of the crowd but as a performer this concert was spot on.

Janet Jackson, Justin Timberlake, Nelly, P. Diddy, Kid Rock, Jessica Simpson

Superbowl XXXVIII Halftime Show, Reliant Stadium, Houston, 1st February 2004

All For You (Janet Jackson)
Mickey (P. Diddy)
Hot In Herre (Nelly)
Bawitdaba (Kid Rock)
Cowboy (Kid Rock)
Rhythm Nation/Rock Your Body
(Janet Jackson with Justin Timberlake)

In a jam-packed line-up of A-listers, 2004's Super-bowl will be mainly remembered for Jackson's boob. At the end of the 'Rhythm Nation' duet with Justin Timberlake, and in front of hundreds of millions of people, Timberlake ripped a piece of Jackson's costume off, exposing a lonely breast. A 'wardobe malfunction' was later blamed as being responsible.

Muse

Glastonbury Festival, Pilton, Somerset
27th June 2004

Hysteria
Newborn
Sing For Absolution
Citizen Erased
Apocalypse Please
Screenager
Sunburn
Butterflies and Hurricanes
Bliss
Time Is Running Out
Plug In Baby
Blackout
Stockholm Syndrome

Frequently regarded as one of *the* live acts of their generation Muse's Sunday headline slot was an awesome achievement for a young band – and a truly remarkable show. Sadly, drummer Dominic's father died shortly after the performance.

Brian Wilson

Royal Festival Hall, London
13th October 2004

One More Summer • Hawaii • In My Room •
Please Let Me Wonder • Good Timing •
You're Welcome • City Full Of People •
Sloop John B • Wouldn't It Be Nice •
God Only Knows • Soul Searchin' •
California Girls • Keep An Eye On Summer •
Catch A Wave • Dance, Dance, Dance •
Don't Worry Baby • Marcella • Sail On Sailor •
Our Prayer • Heroes And Villains • Worms •
Barnyard • Old Master Painter • Sunshine •
Cabinessence • Wonderful • Look •
Child Is Father Of The Man • Surf's Up •
I'm In Great Shape • I Wanna Be Around •
Vegetables • Holidays • Wind Chimes •
Mrs O'Leary's Cow • Water Chant •
Our Prayer (reprise) • Good Vibrations •
I Get Around • Help Me Rhonda • Barbara Ann •
Surfin' USA • Fun, Fun, Fun •
Love And Mercy

The very first performance of Brian Wilson's long-lost masterpiece *Smile*. Paul McCartney, who crunched a carrot on the original recording, was in attendance.

Cream

Royal Albert Hall, London
2nd May 2005

I'm So Glad
Spoonful
Outside Woman Blues
Pressed Rat and Wart Hog Sleepy Time,
NSU
Badge
Politician
Sweet Wine
Rollin' & Tumblin'
Stormy Monday
Deserted Cities Of The Heart
We're Going Wrong
Born Under A Bad Sign
Crossroads
Sitting On Top Of The World
White Room
Toad
Sunshine Of Your Love

A Cream reunion was always something their loyal fans wished for after the band's premature demise in 1968. Despite their alleged differences, Cream quite clearly enjoyed being back together performing on the same stage they had said farewell to their fans on 37 years earlier.

Spinal Tap

Carnegie Hall, New York
4th June 2005

Tonight I'm Gonna Rock You Tonight
Cash On Delivery
Hell Hole
Back From The Dead
Rainy Day Sun
Heavy Duty
Clam Caravan
Sex Farm
Stonehenge
The Majesty Of Rock
Stinkin' Up The Great Outdoors
Rock 'n' Roll Creation
(Listen To The) Flower People
Gimme Some Money
Christmas With The Devil
Bitch School
Break Like The Wind
All The Way Home
Short And Sweet
Big Bottom

Spinal Tap, with their exploding drummers and dodgy stage props are truly legendary rock performers. During 'Stonehenge' midgets in druid costumes danced around a miniature Stonehenge suspended from a coat rack. It was, of course, the evening's highlight. Support came from the Folksmen – Christopher Guest, Mike McKean and Harry Shearer's other fictional band.

Green Day

Milton Keynes Bowl
18th June 2005

American Idiot
Jesus Of Suburbia
Holiday
Are We The Waiting
St Jimmy
Longview
Brainstew
Jaded
Knowledge
Basket Case
She
King For A Day
Shout
Wake Me Up When September Ends
Minority
Maria
Boulevard Of Broken Dreams
We Are The Champions
Time Of Your Life

As their *American Idiot* album and tour hit its peak, Green Day played their biggest UK show. The band clearly revelled in making the most of it – playing Queen's 'We Are The Champions' to drive the point home. It was also voted 'The Best Show On Earth' by *Kerrang!* magazine.

Live8 UK

Hyde Park, London
2nd July 2005

Sgt. Pepper's Lonely Hearts Club Band (Paul McCartney and U2)

Beautiful Day • Blackbird • Vertigo • One • Unchained Melody (U2)

In My Place • Bitter Sweet Symphony • Fix You (Coldplay)

The Bitch Is Back • Fighting • Children (Elton John w/ Pete Doherty)

White Flag • Thank You • Seven Seconds (Dido w/Youssou N'Dour) The Bartender And The Thief • Dakota • Maybe Tomorrow • Local Boy In The Photograph (Stereophonics)

Imitation of Life • Everybody Hurts • Man on the Moon (R.E.M)

Dy-na-mi-tee • Redemption Song (Ms. Dynamite)

Somewhere Only We Know • Bedshaped (Keane)

Sing • Side/Stayin' Alive • Why Does It Always Rain On Me? (Travis)

I Don't Like Mondays (Bob Geldof)

Why • Little Bird • Sweet Dreams (Annie Lennox)

Food for Thought • Who You Fighting For? • Reasons • Red Red Wine • Can't Help Falling in Love (UB40)

Ups & Downs • Drop It Like It's Hot • Signs • The Next Episode • What's My Name • Hey Hey (Snoop Dogg)

Somewhere Else • Golden Touch • In The City (Razorlight)

Like a Prayer • Ray of Light • Music
(Madonna)
Chocolate • Run (Snow Patrol)
All These Things That I've Done
(The Killers)
Super Duper Love • I Had a Dream • Some Kind
of Wonderful (Joss Stone)
Laura • Take Your Mama • Everybody Wants the
Same Thing (Scissor Sisters)
Do It For The Kids, • Fall To Pieces • Slither
(Velvet Revolver)
Message In A Bottle • Driven To Tears • Every
Breath You Take (Sting)
Make It Happen • Hero • We Belong Together
(Mariah Carey)
We Will Rock You • Let Me Entertain You • Feel
• Angels (Robbie Williams)
Who Are You • Won't Get Fooled Again
(The Who)
Speak to Me/ Breathe • Money • Wish You Were
Here • Comfortably Numb (Pink Floyd)
Get Back • Drive My Car (w/ George Michael)
Helter Skelter • The Long And Winding
Road/Hey Jude
(Paul McCartney + ensemble)

With half the world watching various Live8 concerts
that day, the music elite rocked for Bob Geldof
once again.

Coldplay

Glastonbury Festival, Pilton, Somerset
13th July 2005

Square One
Politik
Yellow
God Put A Smile Upon Your Face
Speed Of Sound
Low
Warning Sign
Everything's Not Lost
White Shadows
The Scientist
Till Kingdom Come
Don't Panic
Clocks
Swallowed In The Sea
Can't Get You Out Of My Head
In My Place
Fix You

This gig marked Coldplay's triumphant return to Glastonbury three years after their last Pyramid Stage headline slot. With a nod to Kylie Minogue, who was due to headline on the Sunday but pulled out for health reasons, Coldplay displayed a flawless performance and a fantastic end to the Saturday.

Artic Monkeys

Sheffield Leadmill, Sheffield
22nd January 2006

When The Sun Goes Down
I Bet You Look Good On The Dancefloor
View From The Afternoon
Still Take You Home
You Probably Couldn't See For The Lights But
You Were Looking Straight At Me
Bigger Boys And Stolen Sweethearts
Dancing Shoes
From The Ritz To The Rubble
Perhaps Vampires Is A Bit Strong But...
Leave Before The Lights Come On
Mardy Bum
Fake Tales Of San Francisco
A Certain Romance

This low-key show at the Sheffield Leadmill coincided with 'When The Sun Goes Down' being the second Number One for the Monkeys. During the performance, Alex Turner asked for the doors to be opened so the people outside who were turned away from entering could hear them play.

Foo Fighters

Hyde Park, London
17th June 2006

In Your Honour
All My Life
Best Of You
Times Like These
Learn To Fly
Breakout
Shake Your Blood (w/ Lemmy of Motörhead)
Stacked Actors
My Hero
Generator
D.O.A.
Monkey Wrench
We Will Rock You
(w/ Brian May and Roger Taylor of Queen)
Everlong
The One

In front of 85,000 fans, and eleven years after the Foo's first sweaty gig, this Hyde Park show has become the band's definitive live highlight. Frontman Dave Grohl later claimed it to be 'the most unbelievable show' of his life.

Madonna

Millennium Stadium, Cardiff

30th July 2006

Future Lovers / I Feel Love
Get Together
Like A Virgin
Jump
Live To Tell
Forbidden Love
Isaac
Sorry
Like It Or Not
Sorry Video Reprise
I Love New York
Ray Of Light
Let It Will Be
Drowned World/Substitute For Love
Paradise (Not for Me)
Music / Disco Inferno (Medley)
Erotica
La Isla Bonita
Lucky Star
Hung Up

Starting in May 2006, Madonna's *Confessions* Tour set the record by a female artist by grossing over $260 million. Sixty shows, 1.2 million people in attendance and, as with most things Madonna does, plenty of media controversy.

Rolling Stones

Copacabana, Rio de Janeiro
18th February 2006

Jumping Jack Flash
It's Only Rock 'n' Roll
You Got Me Rocking
Tumbling Dice
Oh No Not You Again
Wild Horses
Rain Fall Down
Midnight Rambler
Night Time Is The Right Time
This Place Is Empty
Happy
Miss You
Rough Justice
Get Off Of My Cloud
Honky Tonk Women
Sympathy For The Devil
Start Me Up
Brown Sugar
You Can't Always Get What You Want
Satisfaction

What do you get if you stick one million people on a beach with the Rolling Stones? The biggest gig ever – in every sense. Documented as the largest audience ever for a rock concert, the Stones matched the Brazilian audience for flair and style and stormed the event with a brilliant setlist of old and new songs.

Take That

Metro Radio Arena, Newcastle Upon Tyne
24th April 2006

Once You've Tasted Love
Pray
Today I've Lost You
Why Can't I Wake Up With You
It Only Takes A Minute
Babe
Everything Changes
Million Love Songs
Beatles Medley
How Deep Is Your Love
Love Ain't Here Anymore
Sure
Relight My Fire (w/ Beverley Knight)
Back For Good
Could It Be Magic (w/ Robbie Williams hologram)
Never Forget

Take That's comeback, ten years after originally causing so much teenage heartbreak, proved to be an unequivocal success. With Robbie Williams especially re-recording his vocals for 'Could It be Magic' he 'performed' as a 10ft hologram for the show, as he was 'unable' to be there in person.

Katie Melua

Troll Offshore Gas Platform, off Norway, North Sea
1st October 2006

Shy Boy
Nine Million Bicycles
Piece By Piece
It's Only Pain
Spiders Web
On The Road Again
I Cried for You
My Aphrodisiac Is You
The Closest Thing To Crazy

It may sound like the closest thing to crazy, but the award for deepest underwater concert record now belongs to Katie Melua and her band. Performing 303m below sea level on the Statoil Troll A gas rig in the North Sea, Melua entertained the rig's workers with this set. The gig, like the nine-minute long elevator down to the makeshift stage, went down a treat.

Patti Smith

CBGBs, New York

15th October 2006

Piss Factory • The Hunter Gets Captured by the Game • Kimberly/The Tide is High • Pale Blue Eyes • Marquee Moon • We Three • Distant Fingers • Without Chains • Ghost Dance • Birdland • Sonic Reducer • Redondo Beach • Free Money • Pissing in a River • Gimme Shelter • Space Monkey • Blitzkrieg Bop/Beat on the Brat/Do You Remember Rock 'n' Roll Radio? /Sheena is a Punk Rocker • Ain't it Strange • So You Want to Be (A Rock 'N' Roll Star) • Babelogue/Rock n Roll Nigger/Little Johnny Jewel • Happy Birthday • For Your Love • My Generation • Land • Gloria • Elegie

The closing night of the legendary New York punk club, CBGBs, was to many, the end of a defining era in punk rock's chaotic history. But who better to give the club a decent farewell than the club's famous first lady.

136

Prince

Superbowl XLI Halftime Show, Dolphin Stadium, Florida
4th February 2007

We Will Rock You
Let's Go Crazy
Baby I'm A Star
Proud Mary (w/ Shelby Johnson)
All Along the Watchtower
Best of You
Purple Rain

With heavy rain visibly drenching the stage, Prince – with his famous purple TAFKAP-logo guitar – ran through a twelve-minute medley of covers before closing with 'Purple Rain'. It has been described as one of 'the greatest half-time shows ever' in part due to Prince's stunning guitar solo-ing.

Elton John
Madison Square Garden, New York
25th March 2007

Sixty Years On • Madman Across The Water •
Where To Now, St. Peter • Hercules •
Ballad of a Well-Known Gun • Take Me To The
Pilot • High Flying Bird • Holiday Inn •
Burn Down The Mission • Better Off Dead •
Levon • Empty Garden • Daniel • Honkey Cat •
Rocket Man • I Guess That's Why They Call It
The Blues • The Bridge • Roy Rogers • Mona
Lisas And Mad Hatters • Sorry Seems To Be The
Hardest Word • Bennie and the Jets •
All The Young Girls Love Alice • Tiny Dancer •
Something About The Way You Look Tonight •
Philadelphia Freedom • Sad Songs (Say So Much) •
Don't Let The Sun Go Down On Me •
I'm Still Standing • The Bitch Is Back •
Crocodile Rock • Saturday Night's Alright For
Fighting • Funeral For A Friend / Love Lies
Bleeding • Your Song

Celebrating his 60th Madison Square Garden performance (the most played by any artist) and his 60th
birthday all in one, Elton John threw a party that no
one would dare forget. Dedicating the song 'Empty
Garden' to John Lennon – a song that Elton only
ever plays in New York in tribute to their last gig
together. (see gig on page 51)

George Michael

Wembley Stadium, London
9th June 2007

Song To The Siren
Fastlove
Too Funky
Father Figure
Everything She Wants
Flawless
You Have Been Loved
Praying For Time
Star People
Shoot The Dog
Outside
Spinning The Wheel
Idol
Jesus To A Child
Faith
I'm Your Man
Amazing
Edge Of Heaven
Careless
Whisper
Freedom '90

As the first performer to christen the new Wembley Stadium, George Michael made sure he didn't disappoint. Despite the lack of a duet, for which many A-listers were mooted, the ex-WHAM! star wowed the crowd with a hit-laden set.

THE BEST GIG I'VE EVER SEEN

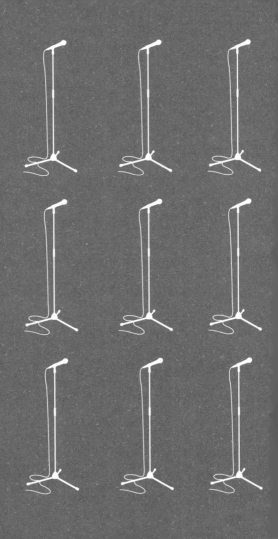

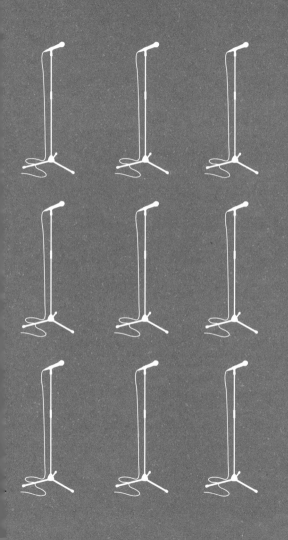